# Beethoven
# Piano Concerto No.2
# in Bb major, Op.19

3002

**MMO CD 3002**

**Music Minus One**

# BEETHOVEN

*Piano Concerto No. 2 in Bb major, Opus 19*

## COMPLETE PERFORMANCE

|          |                       | Band | Page |
|----------|-----------------------|------|------|
| 1st mvt. | Allegro               | 1    | 3    |
| 2nd mvt. | Adagio                | 2    | 26   |
| 3rd mvt. | Rondo - Molto Allegro | 3    | 34   |

## ORCHESTRAL ACCOMPANIMENT

|          |                       | Band | Page |
|----------|-----------------------|------|------|
| 1st mvt. | Allegro con brio      | 4    | 3    |
| 2nd mvt. | Adagio                | 5    | 26   |
| 3rd mvt. | Rondo - Molto Allegro | 6    | 34   |

It was customary in Beethoven's day for the soloist to improvise a virtuosic passage as a climax to the movement before the final orchestral tutti. The passage would incorporate themes from the music and would have a rhapsodic air, often modulating to extreme keys. We have recorded here a typical example that sounds as if Beethoven himself were playing. We invite you to take inspiration from our soloist's lead and improvise your own cadenza. A pause of 8 seconds is inserted at the appropriate point, if you need longer, have your CD remote control handy and make use of the pause button!

# Piano Concerto No. 2

L. van Beethoven, Op. 19.

8

8 seconds are allowed for the Cadenza
in the 'orchestra only' version.

## Music Minus One PIANO Compact Discs

___ MMO CD 3001  Beethoven Piano Concerto No. 1 in C, Opus 15
*MMO CD 3002  Beethoven Piano Concerto No. 2 in Bb, Opus 19
___ MMO CD 3003  Beethoven Piano Concerto No. 3 in Cm, Opus 37
*MMO CD 3004  Beethoven Piano Concerto No. 4 in G, Opus 58
*MMO CD 3005  Beethoven Piano Concerto No. 5 in Eb, Opus 73
___ MMO CD 3006  Grieg Piano Concerto in A minor, Opus 16
___ MMO CD 3007  Rachmaninoff Piano Concerto No. 2 in C minor
*MMO CD 3008  Schumann Piano Concerto in A minor, Opus 54
*MMO CD 3009  Brahms Piano Concerto No. 1 in D minor, Opus 15
___ MMO CD 3010  Chopin Piano Concerto No. 1 in Em, Opus 11
*MMO CD 3011  Mendelssohn Piano Concerto No. 1 in Gm, Opus 25
___ MMO CD 3012  W.A. Mozart Piano Concerto No. 9 in A, K.271
___ MMO CD 3013  W.A. Mozart Piano Concerto No. 12 in A, K.414
*MMO CD 3014  W.A. Mozart Piano Concerto No. 20 in Dm, K.466
___ MMO CD 3015  W.A. Mozart Piano Concerto No. 23 in A, K.488
___ MMO CD 3016  W.A. Mozart Piano Concerto No. 24 in Cm, K.491
*MMO CD 3017  W.A. Mozart Piano Concerto No. 26 in D, 'Coronation'
___ MMO CD 3018  W.A. Mozart Piano Concerto in G major, K.453
*MMO CD 3019  Liszt Piano Concerto No. 1/Weber Concertstucke
*MMO CD 3020  Liszt Piano Concerto No. 2/Hungarian Fantasia
___ MMO CD 3021  J.S. Bach Piano Concerto in Fm/J.C. Bach Concerto in Eb
___ MMO CD 3022  J.S. Bach Piano Concerto in D minor
___ MMO CD 3023  Haydn Piano Concerto in D major
*MMO CD 3024  Heart Of The Piano Concerto
*MMO CD 3025  Themes From The Great Piano Concerti
___ MMO CD 3026  Tschiakowsky Piano Concerto No. 1 in Bbm, Opus 23
*Available Spring 1995

## Music Minus One VOCALIST Compact Discs

___ MMO CD 4001  Schubert Lieder for High Voice
___ MMO CD 4002  Schubert Lieder for Low Voice
___ MMO CD 4003  Schubert Lieder for High Voice  volume 2
___ MMO CD 4004  Schubert Lieder for Low Voice  volume 2
___ MMO CD 4005  Brahms Lieder for High Voice
___ MMO CD 4006  Brahms Lieder for Low Voice
___ MMO CD 4007  Everybody's Favorite Songs for High Voice
___ MMO CD 4008  Everybody's Favorite Songs for Low Voice
___ MMO CD 4009  Everybody's Favorite Songs for High Voice  volume 2
___ MMO CD 4010  Everybody's Favorite Songs for Low Voice  volume 2
___ MMO CD 4011  17th/18th Century Italian Songs High Voice
___ MMO CD 4012  17th/18th Century Italian Songs Low Voice
___ MMO CD 4013  17th/18th Century Italian Songs High Voice  volume 2
___ MMO CD 4014  17th/18th Century Italian Songs Low Voice  volume 2
___ MMO CD 4015  Famous Soprano Arias
___ MMO CD 4016  Famous Mezzo-Soprano Arias
___ MMO CD 4017  Famous Tenor Arias
___ MMO CD 4018  Famous Baritone Arias
___ MMO CD 4019  Famous Bass Arias
___ MMO CD 4020  Hugo Wolf Lieder for High Voice
___ MMO CD 4021  Hugo Wolf Lieder for Low Voice
___ MMO CD 4022  Richard Strauss Lieder for High Voice
___ MMO CD 4023  Richard Strauss Lieder for Low Voice
___ MMO CD 4024  Robert Schumann Lieder for High Voice
___ MMO CD 4025  Robert Schumann Lieder for Low Voice
___ MMO CD 4026  W.A. Mozart Arias For Soprano
___ MMO CD 4027  Verdi Arias For Soprano
___ MMO CD 4028  Italian Arias For Soprano
___ MMO CD 4029  French Arias For Soprano
___ MMO CD 4030  Soprano Oratorio Arias
___ MMO CD 4031  Alto Oratorio Arias
___ MMO CD 4032  Tenor Oratorio Arias
___ MMO CD 4033  Bass Oratorio Arias
John Wustman, Piano Accompanist

## Music Minus One TRUMPET Compact Discs

___ MMO CD 3801  3 Trumpet Concerti  Handel/Telemann/Vivaldi
___ MMO CD 3802  Easy Solos, Student Edition, Beginning Level vol. 1
___ MMO CD 3803  Easy Solos, Student Edition, Beginning Level vol. 2
___ MMO CD 3804  Easy Jazz Duets with Rhythm Section, Beginning Level

## Music Minus One TROMBONE Compact Discs

___ MMO CD 3901  Easy Solos, Student Editions, Beginning Level vol. 1
___ MMO CD 3902  Easy Solos, Student Editions, Beginning Level vol. 2
___ MMO CD 3903  Easy Jazz Duets, Student Editions, 1-3 years

## Music Minus One ALTO SAX Compact Discs

___ MMO CD 4101  Easy Solos, Student Editions, Beginning Level vol. 1
___ MMO CD 4102  Easy Solos, Student Editions, Beginning Level vol. 2
___ MMO CD 4103  Easy Jazz Duets, Student Editions, 1-3 years

## Music Minus One FRENCH HORN Compact Discs

___ MMO CD 3501  Mozart: Concerto No. 2, K.417; No. 3, K.447

## Music Minus One GUITAR Compact Discs

___ MMO CD 3601  Boccherini: Guitar Quintet, No. 4 in D major
___ MMO CD 3602  Giuliani: Guitar Quintet, Opus 65
___ MMO CD 3603  Classic Guitar Duets Easy - Medium

## Music Minus One CELLO Compact Discs

___ MMO CD 3701  Dvorak: Cello Concerto in B minor, Opus 104
___ MMO CD 3702  C.P.E. Bach: Cello Concerto in A minor
___ MMO CD 3703  Boccherini: Concerto in Bb Major; Bruch: Kol Nidrei

## Music Minus One VIOLIN Compact Discs

___ MMO CD 3100  Bruch Violin Concerto in Gm
___ MMO CD 3101  Mendelssohn Violin Concerto in Em
___ MMO CD 3102  Tschaikovsky Violin Concerto in D, Opus 35
___ MMO CD 3103  J.S. Bach "Double" Concerto in Dm
___ MMO CD 3104  J.S. Bach Violin Concerti in Am/E
___ MMO CD 3105  J.S. Bach Brandenburg Concerti Nos. 4 and 5
___ MMO CD 3106  J.S. Bach Brandenburg No. 2/Triple Concerto
___ MMO CD 3107  J.S. Bach Concerto in Dm
*MMO CD 3108  Brahms Violin Concerto in D, Opus 77
*MMO CD 3109  Chausson Poeme/Schubert Rondo
___ MMO CD 3110  Lalo Symphonie Espagnole
___ MMO CD 3111  Mozart Concerto in D/Vivaldi Concerto in Am
___ MMO CD 3112  Mozart Violin Concerto in A, K.219
___ MMO CD 3113  Wieniawski Concerto in D/Sarasate Zigeunerweisen
___ MMO CD 3114  Viotti Concerto No. 22
___ MMO CD 3115  Beethoven Two Romances/"Spring" Sonata
___ MMO CD 3116  St. Saëns Intro & Rondo Cap./Mozart Serenade & Adagio
___ MMO CD 3117  Beethoven Violin Concerto in D major, Opus 61
___ MMO CD 3118  The Concertmaster Solos from Symphonic Works
___ MMO CD 3119  Air On A G String Favorite Encores for Orchestra
___ MMO CD 3120  Concert Pieces For The Serious Violinist
___ MMO CD 3121  Eighteenth Century Violin Music
___ MMO CD 3122  Violin Favorites With Orchestra Vol. 1 (Easy)
___ MMO CD 3123  Violin Favorites With Orchestra Vol. 2 (Moderate)
___ MMO CD 3124  Violin Favorites With Orchestra Vol. 3 (Mod. Diff.)
___ MMO CD 3125  The Three B's: Bach/Beethoven/Brahms
___ MMO CD 3126  Vivaldi Concerti in Am, D, Am Opus 3 No. 6,9,8
___ MMO CD 3127  Vivaldi "The Four Seasons" 2 CD set $29.98 each
___ MMO CD 3128  Vivaldi "La Tempesta di Mare" Opus 8 No. 5
　　　　　　　　　　　　 Albinoni: Violin Concerto in A
___ MMO CD 3129  Vivaldi: Violin Concerto Opus 3 No. 12
*Spring 1995  Vivaldi Violin Concerto Opus 8, No. 6 "Il Piacere"

## Music Minus One FLUTE Compact Discs

___ MMO CD 3300  Mozart Concerto in D/Quantz Concerto in G
___ MMO CD 3301  Mozart Flute Concerto in G major
___ MMO CD 3302  J.S. Bach Suite No. 2 in Bm
___ MMO CD 3303  Boccherini/Vivaldi Concerti/Mozart Andante
___ MMO CD 3304  Haydn/Vivaldi/Frederick "The Great" Concerti
___ MMO CD 3305  Vivaldi/Telemann/Leclair Flute Concerti
___ MMO CD 3306  J.S. Bach Brandenburg No. 2/Haydn Concerto
___ MMO CD 3307  J.S. Bach Triple Concerto/Vivaldi Concerto No. 9
*MMO CD 3308  Mozart/Stamitz Flute Quartets
*MMO CD 3309  Haydn London Trios
*MMO CD 3310  J.S. Bach Brandenburg Concerti No. 4 and No. 5
*MMO CD 3311  W.A. Mozart Three Flute Quartets
*MMO CD 3312  Telemann Am Suite/Gluck 'Orpheus' Scene/Pergolesi Conc. in G
*MMO CD 3313  Flute Song Easy familiar Classics
___ MMO CD 3314  Vivaldi 3 Flute Concerti RV 427, 438, Opus 10 No. 5
___ MMO CD 3315  Vivaldi 3 Flute Concerti RV 440, Opus 10 No. 4, RV 429
___ MMO CD 3316  Easy Solos, Student Editions, Beginning Level vol. 1
___ MMO CD 3317  Easy Solos, Student Editions, Beginning Level vol. 2
___ MMO CD 3318  Easy Jazz Duets, Student Editions, 1-3 years
*Spring 1995

## Music Minus One CLARINET Compact Discs

___ MMO CD 3201  Mozart Clarinet Concerto in A major
*MMO CD 3202  Weber Clarinet Concerto No. 1 in F minor, Op. 73
　　　　　　　　　　　　 Stamitz Clarinet Concerto No. 3 in Bb major
*MMO CD 3203  Spohr Clarinet Concerto No. 1 in C minor, Op. 26
*MMO CD 3204  Weber Clarinet Concertino, Opus 26
___ MMO CD 3205  First Chair Clarinet Solos Orchestral Excerpts
___ MMO CD 3206  The Art Of The Solo Clarinet Orchestral Excerpts
*MMO CD 3207  Mozart: Quintet for Clarinet and Strings in A, K.581
___ MMO CD 3208  Brahms: Sonatas Opus 120, Nos. 1 & 2
___ MMO CD 3209  Weber: Grand Duo Concertant - Wagner: Adagio
___ MMO CD 3210  Schumann Fantasy Pieces, Opus 73, Three Romances
___ MMO CD 3211  Easy Clarinet Solos, Student Editions 1-3 years
___ MMO CD 3212  Easy Clarinet Solos, Student Editions 1-3 years, vol. 2
___ MMO CD 3213  Easy Jazz Duets, Student Editions, 1-3 years
*Available Spring 1995

## Music Minus One OBOE Compact Discs

___ MMO CD 3400  Albinoni Three Oboe Concerti Opus 7 No. 3, No. 6, Opus 9 No. 2
___ MMO CD 3401  3 Oboe Concerti: Handel, Telemann, Vivaldi
___ MMO CD 3402  Mozart/Stamitz Oboe Quartets in F major (K.370; Op.8 #3)

## Music Minus One TENOR SAX Compact Discs

___ MMO CD 4201  Easy Tenor Sax Solos, Student Editions, 1-3 years
___ MMO CD 4202  Easy Tenor Sax Solos, Student Editions, 1-3 years
___ MMO CD 4103  Easy Jazz Duets with Rhythm Section, Beginning Level

## Music Minus One BROADWAY Shows

| | |
|---|---|
| ___ MMO CD 1016  Les Mis/Phantom | ___ MMO CD 1178  The King And I |
| ___ MMO CD 1067  Guys And Dolls | ___ MMO CD 1179  Fiddler On The Roof |
| ___ MMO CD 1100  West Side Story | ___ MMO CD 1180  Carousel |
| 　　　　　　　　　　(2 CD set) | ___ MMO CD 1181  Porgy And Bess |
| ___ MMO CD 1110  Cabaret | ___ MMO CD 1183  The Music Man |
| ___ MMO CD 1173  Camelot | ___ MMO CD 1184  Showboat |
| ___ MMO CD 1174  My Fair Lady | ___ MMO CD 1186  Annie Get Your Gun |
| ___ MMO CD 1175  Oklahoma | ___ MMO CD 1187  Hello Dolly |
| ___ MMO CD 1176  The Sound Of Music | ___ MMO CD 1189  Oliver (2 CD set) |
| ___ MMO CD 1177  South Pacific | |